The ELI Readers collection is a complete range of books and plays for readers of all ages, ranging from captivating contemporary stories to timeless classics. There are three series, each catering for a different age group; Young ELI Readers, Teen ELI Readers and Young Adult ELI Readers. The books are carefully edited and beautifully illustrated to capture the essence of the stories and plots. The readers are supplemented with 'Focus on' texts packed with background cultural information about the writers and their lives and times.

The FSC certification guarantees that the paper used in these publications comes from certified forests, promoting responsible forestry management worldwide.

For this series of ELI graded readers, we have planted 5000 new trees.

Jack London

THE CALL OF THE WILD

Adaptation and activities by Silvana Sardi

Illustrated by Marco Somà

Teen ELI Readers

The Call of the Wild
Jack London
Adaptation and activities by Silvana Sardi
Illustrated by Marco Somà

Language Level Consultants
Janet Borsbey and Ruth Swan

ELI Readers
Founder and Series Editors
Paola Accattoli, Grazia Ancillani, Daniele Garbuglia (Art Director)

Graphic Design
Sergio Elisei

Layout
NoCode - Torino

Production Manager
Francesco Capitano

Photo credits
Corbis, Shutterstock

P.O. Box 6
62019 Recanati (MC)
Italy
T +39 071750701
F +39 071977851
info@elionline.com
www.elionline.com

Typeset in 13 / 18 pt Monotype Dante

Printed in Italy by Tecnostampa Recanati - ERT 323.01
ISBN 978-88-536-1577-0

First edition: February 2013

www.elireaders.com

Contents

These icons indicate the parts of the story that are recorded **start** ▶ **stop** ■

Characters

Buck

Spitz

Dave

Sol-leks

François
Perrault
Charles
Mercedes
Hal
John Thornton

Before you read

Writing

1 Look at the picture and complete the words.

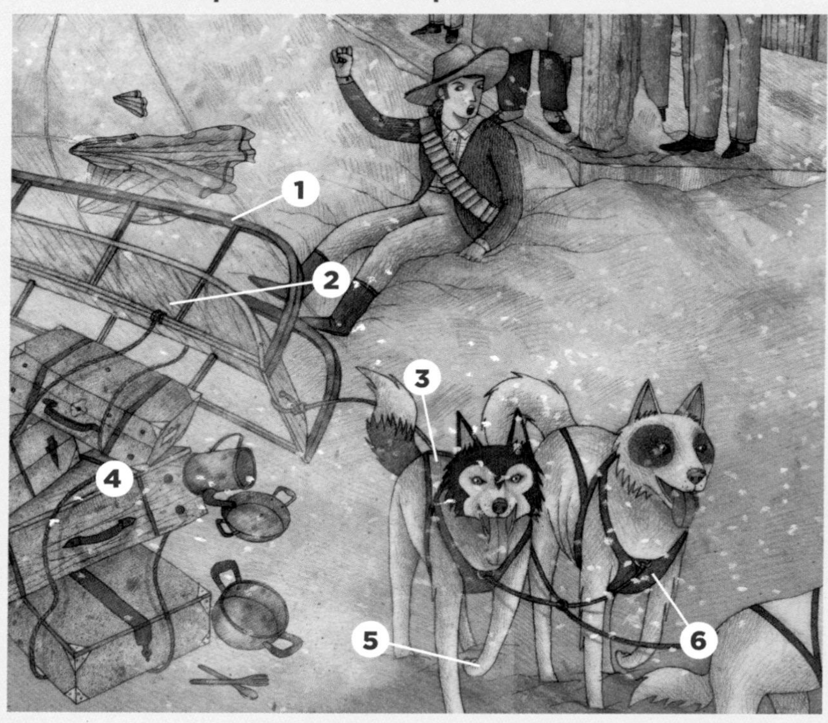

1 R_N_E_S	runners
2 S_ _D	load
3 _US_Y D_G	harness
4 _O_D	husky dog
5 PA_	paw
6 _A_ _ESS	sled

Grammar

2 Underline the correct alternative and complete the text.

The Call of the Wild (**1**) <u>is</u>/*speaks* a story about a dog (**2**) *called/name* Buck. At the beginning of the story, Buck is living (**3**) *in/on* California with Judge Miller and his family. He has a happy life and (**4**) *don't/doesn't* have to worry about (**5**) *nothing/anything*. Then, everything changes and Buck finds (**6**) *him/himself* in the north of Canada. Now he is a working dog, Buck has to learn (**7**) *to pull/pulling* a sled with a team (**8**) *of/from* husky dogs. Life in the cold North is (**9**) *hardly/hard* and (**10**) *very/much* different from his old one.

Word-building

3a Complete the table. Use a dictionary if necessary.

Adjective	Noun
	anger
beautiful	
dangerous	*danger*
	friendliness
frightened	
happy	
	hunger
thirsty	

3b Choose the correct alternative in the sentences below. Use the table to check your answers.

1 Buck's life in California is very <u>happy</u>/*happiness*.
2 He lives in a *beautiful/beauty* house.
3 His new life in the north is full of *dangerous/danger*.
4 Sometimes he is *thirsty/thirst*.
5 He finds it difficult to control his *hungry/hunger*.
6 When he wakes up he has a *frightened/fright*.

Chapter 1

Far from Home

▶ 2 Buck, a big strong dog, lived happily in a beautiful farmhouse with Judge Miller and his family. He lived in the Santa Clara Valley, near San Jose, California. The land was good in this area and famous for its fruit. Buck was a friendly dog and he loved going fishing with Judge Miller's sons. Life was fun, but things were about to change for Buck. The Klondike* Gold Rush* had started, and Buck would soon be part of it.

All the newspapers were talking about the Gold Rush, but of course Buck couldn't read, so he didn't know anything about it. He wasn't interested in gold anyway!

The Miller family had lots of dogs, but at four years old, Buck was already boss. All the other dogs respected him and every member of the

The Klondike a region of the Yukon (Canada)
Gold Rush a time when lots of people were looking for gold

family loved him too. In summer, the Judge's grandchildren rode on his back, while in winter he sat quietly with Judge Miller in the library in front of a warm fire, where he felt safe and loved. He often walked with the Judge's daughters, and even swam with the boys in the pool in the garden.

Buck wasn't fat like some pets, he loved swimming and became stronger every day. Everybody loved Buck. Unfortunately, the gold-seekers* in the north needed a dog like him. Manuel, the gardener's helper, decided to sell Buck to make a few dollars. So, one evening, he took Buck for a walk when nobody was looking. Buck knew Manuel well and was happy to go with him. They went to the train station, where another man was waiting to give Manuel the money for Buck. The stranger put a rope* round Buck's neck and pulled it tight. Then the man put Buck on a train. The dog was very angry and bit the man's hand, but it was no use, he couldn't escape.

They reached San Francisco where the man gave Buck to another stranger. By now, Buck was very thirsty and hungry. He was even too tired to fight when they cut off his collar and threw him

a gold-seeker a person looking for gold
a rope a piece of very thick string

into a wooden crate*. He couldn't understand what was happening. "Why are they doing this to me?" he thought.

During the night, the man came to see Buck. Buck thought it was the judge, but barked* angrily when he realized it was the stranger. "Where is my master?" he thought sadly.

Next morning, four men came for the dog. They looked dangerous and Buck barked at them from inside the crate. They just laughed at him and put the crate on another train.

Buck now began a long journey which took him far from the peace and quiet of his home and the people who loved him. From the train, they moved him to a truck, then a boat, then finally a train once more. All this time, nobody gave Buck even a drink of water and he was weak and frightened.

Two days and nights passed, and Buck lay in the crate barking when anyone came near him. He was really thirsty now, and he was furious* with these men who were taking him away from everything he knew and loved. His eyes were red, he was dirty and angry, and he didn't look like

a crate a wooden box (see picture on p. 15)
to bark to make the loud sound a dog makes
furious very, very angry

the Buck Judge Miller knew. He couldn't wait to get out of the crate to try and bite these men. He no longer had the rope around his neck, but his throat hurt.

At last they reached Seattle, and the four men carried the crate into a small back yard* with high walls. Then, a man with a red sweater came into the back yard. He was carrying a hatchet* in one hand and a club* in the other. Buck knew he was in danger. The man hit the wooden crate with the hatchet to open it, and inside Buck pushed angrily against the breaking wood. He wanted out. He was like a wild animal, ready to attack.

"Come on then, red eyes," said the man, as he hit the crate once more and broke it open.

Buck jumped at him with a mad look in his eyes. The man hit Buck hard with the club and the dog fell to the ground. Buck tried again, but it was no use. Each time, the man in the red sweater hit him with the club. The man continued to hit Buck until the dog lay on the ground. When Buck looked up, the man was standing over him.

"Well, Buck", he said, "now you know who is boss. Be a good dog and you won't have any problems."

a back yard an area behind a building (see picture on p. 15)
a hatchet a tool for cutting wood (see picture on p. 15)
a club a big heavy stick

Then the man gave the dog some food and water. Buck had to accept that he couldn't fight against a club and a hatchet, he realized that now. This was the first lesson he learned in this new world.

Every day, new dogs arrived, and the man in the red sweater was ready for them with his club. Sometimes men came, gave the man some money and took a dog away.

"I wonder where they are going?" thought Buck.

Then, one day, a little man who spoke French came and chose Buck. The man was Perrault and he delivered letters and parcels for the Canadian government. He needed a strong dog to pull the mail sled* and Buck was perfect for the job. The man also bought another dog called Curly. He took the two dogs to the ship, where his friend François was waiting. There were another two dogs there, and they left for the cold North. The other dogs were called Spitz and Dave. Spitz was a big white dog who tried to steal Buck's dinner the first night. François punished Spitz, so Buck decided that this new master was a good man.

a sled the dogs are pulling one in the picture on p. 23

The other dog, Dave, was very quiet and wasn't interested in Buck and Curly.

As they went north, it got colder and colder. Then, early one morning, they arrived at Dyea beach, near Skaguay, in Alaska. This was where a lot of gold-seekers began their journey to the goldfields around Dawson in the Yukon, Canada.

After-reading Activities

Reading

1 Match each description to the right person.

1 [f] He had a farmhouse in California.
2 [ ] He sold Buck for a few dollars.
3 [ ] Buck bit his hand.
4 [ ] He hit Buck with a club.
5 [ ] He took Buck to the ship.
6 [ ] He punished Spitz for trying to steal Buck's dinner.

a The stranger
b Manuel
c François
d The man in the red sweater
e Perrault
f Judge Miller

Grammar

2 Underline the correct alternative.

1 Buck loved *fishing/fish* with Judge Miller's boys.
2 Buck couldn't *read/to read* about the gold rush.
3 Manuel wanted *sell/to sell* Buck.
4 Buck liked *swimming/swim* in the pool.
5 Buck hated *being/be* in the crate.
6 The man in the red sweater decided *to give/giving* Buck some food.
7 Buck learned *be/to be* a good dog.

Vocabulary

3 Circle the odd word out.

1	loved	enjoyed	(hated)	liked
2	happy	furious	angry	worried
3	thirsty	friendly	hungry	tired
4	car	truck	train	boat
5	warm	strong	thin	fat

Preliminary - Writing

4 Imagine you are Perrault. Write a letter to your boss and tell him about the new dog you have bought. Tell your boss:

- where you bought the dog
- why you chose him
- when you plan to leave

Write 35-45 words.

Before-reading Activity

Listening and Speaking

5a At the end of chapter 1, Buck arrives in Alaska. What will happen now? Work in pairs. Read the following sentences and decide if they are true (T) or false (F).

		T	F
1	Buck finds everything strange.	☑	☐
2	Buck is happy to leave the ship.	☐	☐
3	There is snow on the ground.	☐	☐
4	The dogs from the other teams are friendly.	☐	☐
5	Spitz helps Curly.	☐	☐
6	Spitz and Buck become friends.	☐	☐

▶ 3 **5b Now listen to the start of chapter 2 and check your answers.**

Chapter 2

A Dog's Life

3 After so many days at sea, Buck was glad when François took them off the ship. Everything was bright and his paws* touched something soft, white and cold – snow! The others laughed when Buck seemed to dance and try to catch the snow with his tongue. It had never snowed in the Santa Clara Valley! He felt happy again, but not for long.

There were other men and their dogs. The men showed their clubs and the dogs showed their teeth as soon as Buck went near them. These husky* dogs were like wolves* and ready for a fight at any time. Poor Curly didn't realize this and tried to be friendly. Buck could do nothing to help when a big husky attacked and killed Curly.

Buck was shocked and angry. Spitz laughed, and from that moment, Buck hated him. Then Buck had another shock. François put some belts on him and attached him to a sled.

a paw an animal's foot
a husky a strong sled dog
a wolf a wild dog

▶ 4 "Does he think I'm a horse?" thought Buck, as he pulled François on the sled into the forest. That afternoon, Buck the family pet became Buck the working dog.

Buck quickly learned to pull the sled with the other dogs, even though it was all new and strange for him. Spitz was the leader at the front, while Dave was at the back. The two more experienced* dogs made sure Buck did the job right. François was pleased with Buck too.

While the others were in the forest, Perrault bought two huskies, Billee and Joe to help pull the sled. They were brothers but very different. Billee was good and gentle and Spitz was horrible to him. Joe, however, was always angry, so Spitz didn't touch him.

That evening, a dog called Sol-leks joined the team. He was an old, thin husky with only one eye. Like Dave, he didn't say much, but the other dogs respected him, even Spitz. Now they had a good team to pull the sled to Dawson, with the government letters and parcels.

When night came, Buck didn't know where to sleep. When he tried to get into the tent, Perrault

experienced expert

and François threw pots and pans at him and told him to go away. It was cold and windy. Buck lay down on the snow, but it was too cold, so he walked around the camp, looking for somewhere warmer. "Where are all the others?" he thought.

He was walking sadly around the tents, when suddenly something moved under the snow. Buck jumped back in fear, but relaxed when he realized it was Billee. Billee was in a hole under the snow.

"So this is how they keep warm," Buck thought, and began to dig a hole in the snow for himself. He slept all night in his new bed. When he woke up next morning, he couldn't remember where he was and started to panic because he was covered in snow. He pushed up and out of the hole with all his strength. When he saw the light of day and the camp, he remembered where he was and how much his life had changed.

François saw Buck and said, "Look Perrault! That new dog already knows how to make a bed in the snow!"

"I know," answered Perrault. "He's a clever dog. I'm glad we bought him. He will help us deliver everything quickly."

They bought even more huskies to complete the team and soon the dogs were pulling the sled along the trail* to Dawson. Buck was happy to leave the camp. It was hard work pulling the heavy sled across the snow, but he enjoyed it. All the dogs in the team were excited and they wanted to do a good job. Dave and Sol-leks were very active and got angry if there were any delays. Dave helped Buck as much as he could. Sol-leks gave him instructions too, and soon Buck became an expert sled dog. François and Perrault were pleased with him as well. Sometimes Perrault examined Buck's paws to see if they were alright.

They reached the camp at Lake Bennet late that night. This camp was very big and full of thousands of gold-seekers. Buck was very tired and was soon asleep in his hole in the snow. However, at sunrise, they woke him again and he was soon back at work in the cold, pulling the sled with his mates.

Day after day, they travelled over ice and snow. François and Perrault were experts at their job and carefully guided their team of dogs over the ice. Sometimes it was dangerous, because the

a trail (here) a route in the snow

ice was thin. They always started when it was dark, and didn't stop until it was dark again in the evening.

Every night they gave the dogs some fish to eat, but it was not enough for Buck and he was always hungry. He learned to eat fast, because the other dogs tried to steal his food. He watched the other dogs and learned their habits. One night, Pike, one of the new dogs, stole a slice of bacon while Perrault wasn't looking.

The night after, Buck stole a lot more bacon. He was so quick that François blamed one of the other dogs. He was learning fast how to stay alive in this new, difficult world. When he had lived with Judge Miller, he had never stolen anything, but now it was different: this new life was full of men with clubs, and dogs with sharp teeth.

As the days passed, Buck became fitter and stronger. He learned to eat everything, even if it was disgusting. He was no longer the Judge's pet who only ate what he liked. Here, he needed food to live. He could see, smell and hear better and even when he was sleeping, he could sense* if there was danger. He learned to clean the ice

to sense to feel, to understand

from his toes to stop them freezing. He learned to break the top of the ice to drink the water under it. He learned to understand the direction of the cold wind, to choose the best place to sleep. He learned all these new things from experience and from natural instinct*. Buck was now almost like a wolf and at night he pointed his nose towards the stars in the sky and howled* like a wolf.

Despite learning all these new things, Buck was still Buck. He was patient and quiet, he didn't fight with the other dogs, not even with Spitz. Spitz didn't like Buck's self-control and he tried again and again and again to make Buck angry. But Buck always stayed calm.

Then, one night, Spitz went too far. It had been a hard day; very windy and with a lot of snow. The dogs were exhausted*, so the team stopped to camp near a lake. All the dogs looked for nice places to sleep. Buck found himself a very good place near some rocks. Then he heard François calling him for his fish and he ran to get his supper. When he went back to his bed, Spitz was there; there in Buck's bed. Buck was furious.

François was still feeding the other dogs when

an instinct a natural feeling
to howl to cry like a dog or wolf
exhausted very, very tired

he suddenly saw Buck attack Spitz. "Go on Buck!" he cried. "Teach that dirty thief a lesson!"

Buck and Spitz were fighting hard. All the other dogs were watching the fight. Nobody saw and nobody knew, but something much more dangerous was about to happen. A large group of mad dogs was about to attack the camp.

Grammar

1 Complete the sentences with the correct comparative form of an adjective from the box.

old warm thin cold disgusting patient difficult ~~nice~~ dangerous fit

1 Billee was *nicer* than Joe because he was gentle.
2 The weather in the north was ________________ than the weather in California.
3 Buck's life now was __________ than the easy life he had had on the farm.
4 Sol-leks was ________________ than Buck who was only four years old.
5 Buck looked for a ________________ place to sleep than on top of the cold snow.
6 Life in the north was ________________ than his safe life in the south.
7 The ice on the lake was ________________ in some places than in others.
8 Buck worked hard and got ___________ every day, so he didn't feel tired anymore.
9 Buck's food was ________________ than it had been in California.
10 Buck was __________ than the other dogs. He waited and had more self-control than Spitz.

Vocabulary

2 Complete the following sentences with a word from the box.

enough	too	much	so	very	~~like~~	such	than

1 The huskies were *like* wolves.
2 Buck was ________ cold that he couldn't sleep.
3 Dave helped Buck as ________ as he could.
4 Lake Bennet camp was a ________ big camp.
5 Buck was tired after ________ a long day and was soon asleep.
6 François didn't have ________ dogs for his team.
7 Buck was smarter ________ the other dogs.
8 Buck was ________ tired to eat and went straight to bed.

Before-reading Activity

Listening

3a At the end of chapter 2, Buck and Spitz start to fight. What will happen now? Work in pairs. Read the following sentences and decide if they are true (T) or false (F).

		T	F
1	The mad dogs have angry red eyes.	☑	☐
2	The mad dogs attack the camp.	☐	☐
3	The mad dogs are fat.	☐	☐
4	Buck and Spitz continue their fight.	☐	☐
5	The mad dogs eat all the food.	☐	☐
6	The mad dogs are stronger than the team dogs.	☐	☐
7	There is no escape across the frozen lake.	☐	☐

▶ 5 **3b Now listen to the start of chapter 3 and check your answers.**

Chapter 3

The Fight

5 Everybody was concentrating on the fight, so nobody saw them coming. A large group of mad husky dogs with angry red eyes attacked the camp. These dogs were very thin and very hungry and there were a lot of them. They attacked; they attacked everything that moved.

Buck and Spitz forgot about their own fight. They started fighting together against these mad attackers. But there were mad dogs everywhere, eating everything they could find. The team dogs tried to fight back, but the wild huskies were too strong for them. The team dogs didn't know where to go; they had the rocks behind them and the frozen lake in front of them. The frozen lake was their only escape.

6 François and Perrault were so busy trying to save the food that they couldn't help the dogs.

"I've had enough of this," thought Billee, and ran away across the ice-covered lake towards the forest. Two of the team dogs followed him, escaping across the ice. Buck tried to follow too, but Spitz pushed him to the ground where the mad huskies could attack him. Luckily, Buck was too quick for them and got onto his feet again. Then he ran after the other team dogs into the forest. Now he hated Spitz even more.

The team dogs hid in the forest. They were all hurt and exhausted. They stayed there until sunrise, then slowly went back to the camp. François and Perrault were waiting for them. They were very angry. The mad dogs had eaten half of the food and some of the sled equipment was damaged. They had even eaten Perrault's shoes! Then François saw *his* dogs. "I hope the bites from those mad dogs don't make all of you mad too!" he said.

Perrault was worried too. They still had to travel four hundred miles* to reach Dawson. He needed strong, healthy dogs, not mad ones!

After two hours, they were ready to go, but the trail was difficult, and the injured dogs moved slowly. They pulled the sled across thirty miles of frozen river. Sometimes the ice was thin and

a mile 1 mile is about 1.6 kilometers

broke under them. Perrault and François had to light a fire and dry their wet dogs. Otherwise the dogs would freeze. It was now fifty degrees below zero.

Buck's paws were soft. The long walk and the snow and ice made them hurt. He could hardly walk because of the pain. He was really hungry, but he couldn't get up for his food and François had to bring it to him. After looking at Buck's paws, François decided to make four shoes for him.

"Ooh that feels good," thought Buck. He wore the shoes until his paws got better and he could walk properly again.

Then another bad thing happened. One morning, one of the dogs, Dolly, suddenly went mad. She tried to attack Buck and Buck had to run. He had to run for his life. Buck ran for miles with the mad dog trying to catch him. François followed. He didn't want to lose Buck. Dolly finally slowed down. François quickly took out his gun and he killed Dolly. He took Buck back to the camp and Buck lay down exhausted. Spitz saw his chance and attacked. Luckily François was there.

He saw Spitz and hit him. Spitz went away angrily.

"One day that Spitz is going to kill poor Buck," said Perrault.

"Don't worry about Buck," said François. "I'm sure he'll teach Spitz a lesson."

From then on, it was open war between the two dogs. Spitz and Buck were enemies, waiting for the right moment to fight. The team finally reached Dawson but after only seven days, they left for Skaguay, again with a full, heavy sled.

The journey to Skaguay was another long one. They stopped and made a camp every night, and the dogs found places to sleep in the snow. The dogs were always hungry. Then one night, a rabbit ran through the camp. The dogs tried to catch it, but the rabbit was too fast for them. They chased after it. Spitz watched the other dogs but did not follow them. He was too clever. He saw where the rabbit was going and he saw a shorter route. He reached the rabbit first, and killed it. Buck was furious and attacked Spitz. They fought hard, rolling on the ground. The other dogs stood around them and watched in silence. They knew that either Buck or Spitz was going to die.

Spitz was a good fighter, but Buck was better. There was no hope for Spitz, and Buck had no pity. He killed Spitz. The other dogs looked at Buck with respect.

Next morning, François and Perrault discovered Spitz dead and Buck badly injured. "I told you Buck was stronger, Perrault!" said François.

"Yes, but Spitz fought hard. Look at Buck, he's injured and he looks bad," answered Perrault.

"Yes, but he's alive," said François. "Now with Spitz dead, we won't have any more problems with the team and we will move faster."

"Yes, you're right!" agreed Perrault.

While Perrault was putting everything on the sled, François got the dogs ready. Buck came and stood in Spitz's place. François didn't notice and put Sol-leks in that position, because he thought he was the best leader they had. Buck was not happy and he pushed Sol-leks away and stood in his place.

"What's this Buck?" asked François. "Don't be silly, you can't take Spitz's place."

He pulled Buck away and put Sol-leks in his place. Again Buck pushed Sol-leks away, but this time François got angry. He hit Buck with his club.

Buck remembered the man in the red sweater and stepped back. François put Sol-leks back in lead position and this time Buck did nothing, but he was angry. "That place is mine," he thought.

François called Buck to put him in his usual place in front of Dave. "Come on Buck, let's go!" he said, but Buck moved farther away. François tried again and again. He put down his club, thinking Buck was afraid of it. It made no difference. Buck wasn't afraid of the club, he wanted to be leader, that was all.

Perrault and François tried to catch Buck for an hour. They threw their clubs and shouted at him, but it was no use. Finally, François sat down and looked at Perrault. The two men smiled. Buck had won. François moved Sol-leks, giving the leader's position to Buck. At last, he was where he wanted to be. He was head of the team.

Buck quickly learnt his duties as leader and the men realized that he was even better than Spitz. Dave and Sol-leks didn't mind about the change of leader. All they wanted was to work hard and well. The rest of the team worked better too. They didn't fight anymore and everybody worked together to move as fast as they could. François bought two more huskies to add to the team. He was surprised at how quickly Buck taught the new dogs to pull the sled. "That Buck sure is a great dog, eh Perrault?"

"He is indeed," agreed Perrault.

Preliminary - Reading

1 Fill in the gaps in the summary of chapter 3 with the correct words – A, B, C or D.

Nobody (**0**) _B_ the hungry huskies arriving, until they were in the camp and (**1**) __ that time it was too late. After fighting for a bit, Buck (**2**) __ to follow Billee over the frozen ice. Spitz (**3**) __ Buck down but he managed to get up again. The team dogs hid in the forest (**4**) __ the next morning. François and Perrault were waiting for them. They were worried and angry too (**5**) __ their sled equipment was damaged. They still had to travel a long (**6**) __ to get to Dawson and it was very cold: 50° (**7**) __ zero. Buck's paws froze in the snow. He had a fight with Spitz over a rabbit and he (**8**)__. He became lead-dog and learned his new duties quickly. He was (**9**) __ better than Spitz.

	A	B	C	D
0	**A** told	~~**B**~~ noticed	**C** said	**D** realized
1	**A** from	**B** in	**C** by	**D** as
2	**A** must	**B** liked	**C** would	**D** tried
3	**A** pushed	**B** shot	**C** threw	**D** ran
4	**A** for	**B** unless	**C** until	**D** since
5	**A** if	**B** because	**C** though	**D** despite
6	**A** way	**B** trail	**C** road	**D** journey
7	**A** behind	**B** below	**C** with	**D** at
8	**A** gained	**B** earned	**C** beat	**D** won
9	**A** much	**B** enough	**C** quite	**D** very

Vocabulary

2 -ing/-ed adjectives. Cross out the wrong alternative in each sentence.

1 The journey was very *tiring/~~tired~~*.
2 The dogs were very *frightening/frightened* by the fight.
3 The team dogs were all *exhausting/exhausted*.
4 Some of the equipment was *damaging/damaged*.
5 The club wasn't *frightening/frightened* to Buck.
6 François was very *surprising/surprised* at Buck's behavior.

Before-reading Activity

Speaking

3a Buck's life changes again in chapter 4. What do you think happens? Match the beginnings and endings. Discuss your answers in pairs.

1 François and Perrault are happy because
  A ☐ the team is very fast
  B ☐ the team can carry a very heavy load
2 François and Perrault are then sad because
  A ☐ they have a new job
  B ☐ they have no more mail to carry
3 The dogs have three new owners:
  A ☐ two men and a woman
  B ☐ three young men
4 The three new owners are
  A ☐ very kind to the dogs
  B ☐ very unkind to the dogs

3b Now read chapter 4 and check your answers.

Chapter 4

Changing Masters

▶ 7 The team, with Buck as leader, worked well. They travelled forty miles a day and arrived in Skaguay after only fourteen days. It was a record! François and Perrault were proud of their dogs, but they were also sad because it was time to leave them. The men had a new job to do and they couldn't work with Buck and the team anymore. François and Perrault left the team and Buck never saw them again.

The dogs had a new master, a Scottish man, and sacks* of mail to carry back to Dawson. Every day was the same. They left early every morning and pulled the sled until night time. Then they ate their fish and went to sleep. Sometimes Buck sat in front of the camp fire after eating and thought about all of his adventures. This new life was no longer strange to him.

When they finally got to Dawson, the dogs had no time to rest. After two days, they left again to go back to Skaguay with other dog teams and their drivers. This time they had letters from the

a sack a very big bag

gold-seekers for their families and friends. The weather was bad and it snowed every day. It was very difficult for the dogs to pull the heavy sled through soft snow and they were very tired. The new drivers were good to the dogs though, and always fed them first, before making their own dinner. They checked the dogs' paws and tried to help them as much as they could.

Not all the dogs lived. When they arrived in Skaguay again, thirty days later, Dave was dead and the other dogs were thin and exhausted. There were more sacks of mail to deliver, but the dogs were too weak to do the trail again. The drivers decided to sell them.

Two men called Hal and Charles bought the team of dogs. Buck saw them give the Scottish man money and knew that these were his new masters. The two men were from the States. Charles was about forty, with a moustache. Hal was about twenty and wore a belt with a gun and a big knife.

When Buck and his team arrived at Hal and Charles's camp, Buck saw that everything was really untidy and dirty. Did these new owners know anything about camping? Did Hal and Charles know anything about the cold? Did they know anything about dogs? Did they know anything about sleds and camping in the snow? Buck didn't think so; Hal and Charles didn't even know how to put up a tent!

"Oh oh," he thought, "these guys can't even look after themselves. How are they going to look after us?"

There was also a woman at the camp called Mercedes. She was Charles's wife and Hal's sister and as inexperienced as the men.

"All we need is the pet cat and the happy family will be complete!" thought Buck.

Hal and Charles started to throw their things onto the sled. Buck could see that they weren't doing a good job. They didn't organize or plan anything. They just threw everything on. They wanted to take *everything* with them, they didn't understand that there were too many things on the sled and the load was dangerous.

Then, some men from the next camp came to watch the scene. "I don't think it's a good idea to take a tent. It'll be heavy and you won't need it," one of them said to Mercedes.

"Oh no, I must have my tent!" said Mercedes.

"It's spring," said the man, "so it won't be cold."

"No, no," insisted Mercedes, "I must have my tent."

The load was now like a mountain on top of the sled. There were clothes, pots and pans, dishes, everything you could think of and… the tent! The men from the other camp stood watching and smiling. They knew that there was trouble ahead.

The sled was so heavy that the dogs couldn't move it.

"You need to clean the runners*," said the man. "They are frozen in the snow."

Hal did as the man said. The dogs pulled hard and this time, the sled started to move. But now it was going too fast, and, as they took the bend onto the main street, Hal lost control of the sled. The sled began to move from side to side. There was nothing Hal could do and everything started to fall off. Clothes, pots and pans flew down the street, but Buck and the other dogs didn't stop running. The load was lighter now and they ran faster and faster through the town. They didn't even notice that they had lost their driver. Everybody watched

runners pieces of metal on a sled that touch the snow

and laughed; except Hal, Charles and Mercedes of course!

Eventually* the dogs stopped running. The load from the sled was everywhere. Some of the men helped Hal, Charles and Mercedes pick up their things. "Your sled is too heavy," said one of the men. "Don't take all those dishes! You don't need them."

It was true, so Hal, Charles and Mercedes decided to leave lots of their unnecessary things in Skaguay. They also bought six new dogs to complete the team. Buck realized that the new dogs were useless, but there was nothing he could do. He was team leader, but he wasn't the boss. He couldn't do anything to help his team with these stupid new owners. There were now fourteen dogs, but the sled couldn't carry food for fourteen dogs…

Late next morning, Buck led the long team of dogs up the main street. Most of them were still tired and needed a rest, but it was time to go.

Buck knew he couldn't depend on his new masters. At the end of the first day, it took them half the night to make camp. The next morning

eventually after a long time

it took them half the morning to load the sled again. This happened over and over again. Some days they travelled less than ten miles. They didn't know anything about dogs, either. First, they fed the dogs too much. Then, they realized that the dog food was almost finished and they still had a long way to go, so they started giving the dogs less and less to eat. Now, Buck and his team were not only tired, but also very hungry. The new dogs found it even harder than Buck and the more experienced dogs. Eventually, one by one they died, leaving the other dogs to pull the heavy load.

Charles, Hal and Mercedes argued all the time. They were unhappy and tired. They behaved selfishly: they only thought about themselves. They didn't care about the dogs anymore. Mercedes used to cry when Hal hit the dogs. Now she didn't care. She wanted to ride on the sled because *she* was tired. It didn't matter if she made the sled heavier. Hal hit the dogs a lot, but they were exhausted. Buck often fell at the front; he only managed to get up when Hal's club hit him hard.

It was now spring and the weather was beautiful, but they were all too weak to notice. It was sunny and the birds began to sing. You could hear the sound of water as the ice started to melt in the hills. The ice on the river started to melt, too.

After another exhausting morning, they arrived at another man's camp, near a river. The camp belonged to a man called John Thornton. As soon as Hal stopped the sled, the dogs sat down, exhausted. Hal asked John Thornton for some information about the trail.

"You must stop. It's too dangerous to travel on the river. The ice is too thin," said Thornton.

"They said it was too dangerous to reach White River and here we are!" said Hal.

Thornton looked at Hal, but said nothing. He knew the man was a fool.

"Come on Buck! Get up! Off we go to Dawson!" said Hal, hitting the dogs.

Slowly they started to stand up, but not Buck. Hal was furious and hit him again. Buck stayed where he was. Hal hit him again, but still Buck didn't move. His instinct told him there was danger ahead and he was going nowhere.

After-reading Activities

Reading

1 Are these statements true (T) or false (F)? Correct the false statements.

	T	F
1 After François and Perrault, the dogs' next master was Irish.	☐	☐
2 On their journey back to Skaguay, the weather was better than usual.	☐	☐
3 Dave died on the way back to Skaguay.	☐	☐
4 The next three masters were not experts.	☐	☐
5 Charles, Hal and Mercedes didn't always give the dogs enough food.	☐	☐
6 Hal was very kind to the dogs.	☐	☐

Grammar

2 Complete the sentences with the correct comparative form of the adjective in brackets.

1 The load of mail to carry back to Dawson was (heavy) *heavier* than before.

2 The dogs were (tired) __________ than before because they had had no time to rest.

3 The weather was (bad) __________ than the previous month.

4 The load was (light) ___________ and they ran (fast) ___________ and (fast) ___________ through the town.

5 Hal was (young) ___________ than Charles.

Vocabulary

3 Solve the anagrams of things from a sled load, then match them to the definitions below.

~~1~~ top	p o t	**a** ☐	you can cook food in one of these
2 entt	t _ _ _	**b** ☐ 1	a big container for cooking food
3 npa	p _ _	**c** ☐	people often eat food in one of these
4 sidh	d _ _ _	**d** ☐	letters and parcels
5 slohtec	c _ _ _ _ _ _ _	**e** ☐	a very large bag
6 laim	m _ _ _	**f** ☐	you can sleep in one of these
7 skca	s _ _ _	**g** ☐	you wear these

Before-reading Activity

Listening

4a Do you think these events from the next chapter are true or false?

	T	F
1 Thornton helped Buck.	☐	☐
2 Charles attacked Thornton.	☐	☐
3 Hal and Charles left without Mercedes.	☐	☐
4 There was an accident on the ice.	☐	☐
5 Thornton was very kind to Buck.	☐	☐
6 Buck felt very unhappy.	☐	☐

▶ 8 **4b Listen to the first part of chapter 5 and check. Were you right?**

Chapter 5

Love and Respect

8 John Thornton watched the scene. He looked at Buck. The poor dog didn't move and Thornton realized that the dog was more intelligent than his master.

"That's enough!" shouted John Thornton. He pushed Hal to the ground. Mercedes screamed. Charles did nothing, he was too tired. Hal got up and tried to attack Thornton with his knife, but Thornton was stronger than him. He pushed Hal to the ground again. Then he took Hal's knife, cut the harness*, and set Buck free from the sled.

"Now, get out of here, you fools!" shouted Thornton.

Hal stood up and took control of the sled. Mercedes sat on the sled as usual, and Charles

harness (n + v) dogs wear a harness to pull a sled (see picture on p. 23)

followed behind. The rest of the dogs slowly pulled the sled onto the thin ice of the river. Buck watched them moving slowly over the ice, while Thornton checked the dog to see if he had any broken bones.

"You're alright," said Thornton, "you just need a good feed."

He patted* Buck on the head, and Buck and Thornton sat watching the sled in the distance. Suddenly, there was a CRACK! The thin ice opened up, and the sled and dogs disappeared into the freezing water of the river with Hal, Charles and Mercedes. Thornton looked at Buck and said, "I tried to tell them, but they didn't want to listen."

Buck licked* Thornton's hand in agreement and Thornton patted Buck's head again. Buck hadn't felt so safe for a long time, and was happy that this man was now his new master.

9 Buck spent those long spring days with Thornton and his other two dogs beside the river. He needed the rest and soon got stronger. Thornton was kind and his dogs were friendly too. They waited there happily for Thornton's partners to come with a raft*. The raft to take

to pat to touch an animal kindly
to lick to touch something with your tongue (you lick an ice-cream)
a raft a flat wooden boat

them down to Dawson. Thornton spent the days playing with his dogs or talking to them. He loved them as if they were his children and Buck loved and respected him for this.

Sometimes, Thornton pushed Buck playfully, patted him and told him how good, or silly, or lazy he was. Buck just loved these moments of pure happiness. He laughed with his eyes, jumped around Thornton and licked his hand to show his love for him.

"What are you laughing at, you silly dog?" said Thornton. "Come on, tell me," and he pulled Buck to him in a big warm hug*.

Buck was afraid of losing Thornton, like his other good masters, Judge Miller, François and Perrault. Sometimes, he woke up during the night and went to his master's tent to make sure he was still there.

Buck loved Thornton very much, but this didn't stop him following his wild instincts. He never stole from his new master, but he stole from other men in other camps. He never fought with Thornton's dogs, but he fought any other dog in the area if necessary. He was the loving dog at

hug (n + v) to put your arms around someone (see picture on p. 53)

Thornton's feet, but he was also the wild wolf-like dog who loved nature, hunting* and the wild life of the forest. The forest seemed to call Buck to the wild, and it was only Buck's love for Thornton that stopped him going.

Eventually, Thornton's partners, Pete and Hans, arrived with the raft to take them to Dawson.

Buck and Thornton now went everywhere together, and Buck was always ready to help his master. When autumn came, Buck had the chance to repay his master for saving his life. Thornton was taking a boat downriver, where the rapids* were very fast. Pete and Hans were near the river, with Buck. Suddenly, Thornton lost control of the boat and fell into the water. He was going towards the fastest part of the rapids where it was impossible to swim. Buck immediately jumped into the river and soon reached Thornton in the water. Thornton caught Buck's tail, and the dog tried to pull him onto land, but the rapids were too strong. Buck couldn't fight against them. Thornton managed to reach a rock and ordered his dog to go back onto land. Buck fought hard against the power of the water and managed to

to hunt to kill animals for food
rapids dangerous part of a river where the water moves very fast

get out of the river. Pete put a rope around Buck and said, "Now Hans and I can help you pull. Let's try again."

The dog dived back into the water and swam once more to his master. This time, the men managed to pull master and dog to safety with the rope. They were all exhausted.

⋆ ⋆ ⋆

That winter in Dawson, Buck became a hero again, and one of the most famous dogs in the goldfields.

Thornton and his two partners wanted to go East to look for gold, but they needed money for the trip. One evening, the men started talking about their dogs. "My dog can start a sled with a load of five hundred pounds*," said one man.

"So what?" said Thornton. "Buck can start a sled with a thousand-pound load!"

"Well," said a man called Matthewson, "I'll give you a thousand dollars if he does it! Do you want to bet*?"

There was silence, then Thornton said, "Alright, I'll take the bet. Let's go outside and see!"

Everybody went outside. Nobody, except

a pound 1 pound = about 0.45 kg
to bet to try to win money by guessing the winner in a competition

Thornton thought that Buck could pull such a heavy weight.

The sled was waiting for Buck. On it were twenty sacks of flour, each weighing fifty pounds. It was sixty degrees below zero and the runners of the sled were stuck in the hard snow. The men all stood around and bet against Buck.

Thornton harnessed Buck to the sled. Buck sensed the excitement. His instinct told him that this was important for his master, and he wanted to do his best. Thornton put his head near Buck's and spoke to him softly. Then he stood up and shouted, "Now Buck, PULL!"

Buck swung to the right and pulled hard. Then he swung to the left and pulled hard again. The runners broke free from the frozen snow. The men stood with their mouths open. They couldn't believe it! Then Buck pulled forward and slowly, the sled began to move. Thornton ran behind him and the men shouted and clapped. Buck had done it! He had won the bet. The men threw their hats in the air. Thornton sat down beside Buck and hugged him, tears running down his face. Buck sat in the warmth of that hug, happy for his master.

Reading

1 Put the words in the correct order to make questions, then match them to the answers below.

1 ☑ d Thornton / Buck / free with? / cut / What / did
What did Thornton cut Buck free with?

2 ☐ Thornton / with? / fight / Who / did
____

3 ☐ ice? / to / happened / What / the
____

4 ☐ the sled? / happened / to / What
____

5 ☐ Buck / with? / spring / did / Who / spend
____

6 ☐ they / for? / were / Who / waiting
____

7 ☐ kind of / was / Thornton? / What / master
____

8 ☐ like / did / Buck / about / What / the forest?
____

a It broke.
b Thornton and his other two dogs.
c The wild life.
~~**d**~~ Hal's knife.
e It disappeared into the frozen river.
f Kind. He loved his dogs.
g Thornton's partners.
h Hal.

Vocabulary

2 Match the words or expressions that mean the same.

1 ☐ safe	**a** frightened
2 ☐ below	**b** heat
3 ☐ fast	**c** get to
4 ☐ afraid	**d** quiet
5 ☐ reach	**e** under
6 ☐ warmth	**f** quick
7 ☐ silence	**g** secure

Preliminary - Writing

3 Your English teacher has asked you to write a story. Write about 100 words. Your story must have this title

A Ride on a Sled

Before-reading Activity

Speaking

4a Work in pairs. What do you think happens in the final chapter? Say why.

	YES	NO
1 Thornton and Buck use the money to go and look for gold.	☐	☐
2 Thornton sells Buck for three thousand dollars.	☐	☐
3 Buck loves his new life as a rich man's dog.	☐	☐
4 Buck begins to spend more time in the forest.	☐	☐
5 Buck meets a lot of wolves.	☐	☐
6 Buck returns to California to live with Judge Miller.	☐	☐

4b Now read the final chapter. Were you right?

Chapter 6

Back to the Past

10 Buck earned one thousand six hundred dollars for his master that night. Thornton now had enough money to go East with his partners to look for a mysterious mine* full of gold. Nobody really knew if the mine existed or not, but Thornton wanted to find out.

So, early one morning, Thornton, Pete and Hans, Buck, and six other dogs, left for the East on an unknown trail in search of gold. Thornton didn't take much with him. He had his gun and every day he hunted for food. There was no hurry, and he had time to enjoy the journey.

Buck loved hunting, fishing and exploring new places. They travelled from one camp to the next. At each new camp, they stopped for several weeks, and at every stop, the three men broke the ice on the ground and looked for gold in the dirt. The dogs were free to relax. Then, when summer came, they travelled on lakes and up and down rivers on rafts. There were no more sleds to pull.

a mine a place under the ground where people look for metals and minerals

Months passed, and they continued to explore this strange land. There were forests and mountains, lakes and rivers, wild strawberries and beautiful flowers. Every season was special.

When spring came again, they reached a wide valley. Here, the men set up camp and started looking for gold as usual. This time they were lucky. There was gold in the river and there was a lot of it!

They worked hard every day and put the gold into big sacks. Each day they worked, they got richer and richer. The men were excited and happy. At last they were rich!

The dogs had nothing to do. Buck spent a lot of time in front of the fire. He thought about wild dogs in the past, the wild dogs that had once lived in the forest. He imagined what life was like back then, frightening but exciting. Sometimes, he thought he heard the forest calling him: calling him to the wild. He felt worried, but at the same time, he wanted to be there.

He began to spend more and more time in the forest. He loved running through the long lines of trees and green open spaces. He loved to hide behind the bushes and watch the birds all day long. In the forest, he hid among the trees and watched and listened. He loved the smell of the earth and the cool wood of the trees. The thing he loved most was running through the forest at midnight. He ran and listened to the sounds of the forest. He looked for who, or what, was calling him, but found nothing. He didn't know why he did these things; he was simply following his instinct.

One night, he was sleeping in the camp, when suddenly he heard a howl from the forest. This sound was both strange and familiar. It was calling him. He got up and ran silently through the camp to the woods. The howl was near and he stopped running. He came to an open space in the trees. There, in front of him, was a wolf, with its nose pointing up to the sky. Buck made no noise, but the animal could sense he was there and stopped howling.

Buck came out from behind the trees. The wolf was smaller and thinner than him and was afraid. The wolf ran away, but Buck followed him. Buck was curious and he wanted to meet the wolf. Buck slowly went towards him. The small wolf was braver now and he stayed where he was. Buck went up to him and this time they became friends.

They ran together through the trees, crossed the river and into another forest. The sun was now high in the sky. Buck was so happy that he didn't even notice the time passing. He felt free in the wild. Everything felt familiar. He was answering the call of the forest; the call of the wild.

When they stopped to drink, Buck remembered Thornton and decided it was time to go back to the camp. When he arrived, Thornton was having dinner. Buck ran to his master, happy to see him again.

For the next two days and nights, he stayed with Thornton all the time. Then he felt he needed to return to the forest again, but this time the wolf wasn't there. He started staying away from the camp for days and nights. He hunted for food, fished in the river and loved this new wild life. He looked everywhere for his wolf friend, but he had no luck.

Autumn came and Buck now spent most of his time in the forest. He was a good hunter and he hunted like a wolf, but he also used his own intelligence. On one of his trips in the forest he saw a moose*. He hunted the huge animal for four whole days and finally managed to kill it, despite its size. He stayed in the forest for two more days; eating and sleeping. Then he decided to go back to the camp and to Thornton.

As he got nearer the camp, he felt that there was something different in the air. His instinct told him something was wrong. He ran faster and faster towards the camp and got nearer and nearer. Then, suddenly, he heard voices singing a strange song. But the voices weren't those of Thornton, Pete and Hans.

Then, Buck saw them. A group of Yeehats* were dancing around the ruins of Thornton's camp. They had clubs and spears*. They were waving them in the air. Buck understood the terrible truth. Thornton, his master and friend, was gone forever.

Buck first felt pain, then anger, and he attacked the Yeehats without thinking. He didn't care how many there were. He wanted them to pay for what they had done. Buck was so fast and furious that the Yeehats had no time to defend themselves.

a moose a large, North American animal
Yeehats Jack London invented this name (see picture p. 65)
a spear the men in the picture on page 65 are holding spears

They tried to hit Buck with their clubs. They threw their spears at him. But, in the confusion, they hit each other and a lot of the Yeehats died. The others ran back to the woods. They thought Buck was mad and were very frightened of him. Buck ran after them through the forest. He ran for miles and miles. He wanted to kill those Yeehats. He eventually caught some of them and attacked them. Again they ran away and Buck was now exhausted. He went back to the camp.

He found his master, dead, near a tree. He sat there for hours, then walked sadly around the camp. There was nothing there and nobody left alive. There was blood everywhere and spears all over the ground. Buck felt a huge emptiness inside, like hunger, only this emptiness was full of pain. He looked at the dead Yeehats. He was proud of what he had done.

He stayed at the camp all day. He stayed by his master and friend. Then, that night, Buck looked up at the full moon in the dark sky. He knew what he needed to do.

He could see the forest in the light of the moon. He understood that a new life was waiting for him there. He stood up and listened. He could hear the sound of animals. He could hear the forest calling him. This time, there was nobody to stop him going forever. His master was dead. He no longer belonged to man. It was time for him to go back to the woods and live his new life in the wild.

A pack of wolves crossed the river into Buck's valley. They were there to hunt moose. They came through the woods. Buck was standing waiting for them.

Some wolves stopped and looked at Buck. He was like a statue. His coat of fur shone in the moonlight. He was magnificent.

Then one of the wolves tried to attack Buck. Buck was too strong for him and won easily.

Three other wolves tried, one after the other, but they all lost against Buck.

Now the wolves were furious and attacked Buck together. Buck was quick and moved fast. He ran to the river where the old mine was. There was a wall of sand on three sides. He faced the wolves; they couldn't get behind him now. They stood and stared at him, but they knew he was too strong. Eventually, the wolves gave up. Buck was not only stronger than them, but more intelligent.

Then, a small, thin wolf came towards Buck. It was his old friend from the night in the forest. They touched noses. Buck was happy to see him again.

Another older wolf came to Buck and touched noses too. This was to show the others that Buck was now their new leader. Then, the wolf sat down, pointed its nose up to the moon and howled. The other wolves did the same.

Buck felt the same howl inside him. He sat in the same position next to the old wolf. He lifted his nose towards the full moon and howled like the other wolves. This was the call of the wild.

He ran through the forest with the rest of the wolves. He was happy to be where he belonged at last, free and wild in the forest.

After-reading Activities

Reading

1 Read the following sentences about chapter 6 and decide if they are true (T) or false (F).

		T	F
1	Thornton went East with two other men to look for gold.	☑	☐
2	The trail they had to follow to go East was famous.	☐	☐
3	They discovered gold after about a year.	☐	☐
4	The dogs worked hard while the men were digging for gold.	☐	☐
5	Buck wanted to spend more and more time in the forest.	☐	☐
6	Buck was bigger than the wolf he first met in the forest.	☐	☐
7	In autumn, he spent a long time hunting a mouse.	☐	☐
8	Apaches attacked Thornton's camp.	☐	☐
9	Buck didn't arrive in time to save his friends from their attackers.	☐	☐
10	Buck killed a lot of the attackers.	☐	☐
11	At the end of the story, Buck met his wolf friend again.	☐	☐

Writing

2 Did you enjoy *The Call of the Wild*? Write a paragraph explaining why you liked/didn't like the book. Think about:

- the events
- the characters
- how the book made you feel

Vocabulary

3 **Read the clues and complete the crossword.**

Across

2 Buck learns to pull this.
3 Thornton goes ________ to look for gold with Pete and Hans.
7 The drivers feed their dogs with this.
9 The state Buck lives in with Judge Miller.
10 Mercedes wants to take this with her to sleep in.
11 After Spitz dies, Buck wants to be this for the sled team.

Down

1 Wild dogs who live in the forest.
4 The wolves are weaker than Buck - Buck is __________.
5 What men discover in the North.
6 Buck travels to Alaska with Curly on this.
8 Buck sleeps outside in the snow in this.
9 The container Buck travels in to Seattle.

Focus on...

Jack London

Early Life

Jack London was born in the United States on 12th January 1876. His real name was John Griffith Chaney. He lived with his mother Flora and her husband John London in Oakland, USA. John London wasn't his father, but he used this name in the future. His family was not particularly rich, so he started working when he was only 14. He had many adventures in his life.

Jack London's cabin.

Working Life

Jack London's first job was in a factory. Then, when he was 15, he became an oyster pirate, and by the age of 17, he had become a good sailor. When he was 18, he had no money and no home, and spent some time in prison. He got involved in politics when he was 20, and was part of the Oakland Socialist Party. He passionately defended the rights of workers and wrote about their conditions. When he was 21, he went to the Klondike to look for gold. Apart from writing, he also sailed the South Seas in his boat with his wife. He visited many places like the Solomon Islands and Hawaii. Then, at 35, he became an excellent rancher and by the time he was 40 he had become a millionaire. He died on 22nd November 1916, when he was only 40.

Fame as a Writer

Jack London started writing when he was 22 and became a journalist for the American publishing company Hearst. He published a number of short stories in magazines. He soon became a famous author worldwide, when *The Call of the Wild* was published. At that time he was 27 years old. This is not his only book about dogs. One of his other most popular books is *White Fang*. It is the story of a wolf that finally leaves the wild to live with a man and his family. Both books are set during the Klondike Gold Rush. He wrote more than 50 books but his most popular works are his dog stories.

Jack London in Alaska.

Task

Complete the form with the information about Jack London.

Real Name: ______________________

Place of Birth: ______________________

Date of Birth: ______________________

Age Started Work: ______________________

Where: ______________________

Number of Books Written: ______________________

Two Famous Works: ______________________

Date of Death: ______________________

Focus on...

Huskies

A special dog

A Husky is the general name given to a type of dog which is used to pull sleds in cold northern regions. They are energetic and athletic and are famous for being very fast. In fact, they are often used in sled dog racing. They have a thick coat of fur and their eyes can be brown, blue or even yellow. Huskies have been the subject of many films including Balto, Eight Below, and Snow Dogs which are all about sledding.

Balto

Balto was the name of a Siberian husky whose determination and courage saved the lives of many children in Nome, Alaska in 1925. At that time in Nome, there was a terrible disease called diphtheria and Balto and his team of dogs transported the antitoxin, by sled to Nome, to stop this epidemic. Balto became a hero, and a statue of the dog was put up in Central Park in New York in 1925. Every year this event is remembered with the Iditarod Trail Sled Dog Race.

Balto.

Iditarod Trail Sled Dog Race

This sled dog race takes place at the beginning of March and goes from Anchorage to Nome in western Alaska. It usually takes a team of about fourteen dogs between 9 and 15 days to do the journey. They go through forests, across rivers and over mountains and it is very hard work. This race is the most popular sporting event in Alaska and people from all over the world take part every year, including many women.

Skijoring

This is a popular winter sport in Scandinavia, Canada and Russia. A person on skis is pulled by a dog, or dogs. Skijoring races can be short-distance sprints or held over longer distances.

Bikejoring

This is when a dog pulls a person on a bike. This is an out of season sport, when there is no snow. It is often used to train sled dogs for the winter months and they run on soft trails in the countryside.

Many people disagree with using animals in sport. What do you think? Write a paragraph giving your opinion. Think about sledding, hunting, show-jumping, bull-fighting or another sport you know.

Focus on...

The Klondike Gold Rush

The Klondike Region

The Klondike is a region in northwest Canada and is part of the Yukon Territory. This region has a subarctic climate, so it's extremely cold in winter. It usually snows from September to May and the rivers are covered in ice from October till spring.
Dawson city is on the Klondike River. It became famous worldwide for the Klondike Gold Rush in 1896. At this time, the population of Dawson grew to forty thousand. Then, after the Gold Rush ended in 1899, it went back to being a small town of 8,000 people.

The Gold Rush

During the Gold Rush, between 1897 and 1899, more than 100,000 people went to the Klondike region to look for gold.
Gold was discovered there for the first time in August 1896, along the Klondike River. When gold started to arrive in the ports in Northwest America, people from Seattle and San Francisco heard about it, and rushed to the region in the hope of becoming rich. Newspapers started writing about the discovery of large quantities of gold, so lots of people left their jobs to go and dig for gold. It was a long hard journey to the Klondike, and they had to cross mountain passes with heavy loads. The lucky ones discovered mines full of gold, but the majority arrived too late. The gold rush in this region lasted until 1899. Then, gold was discovered in Nome, Alaska, so everybody moved there.

Trails

Most people arrived in South-east Alaska at the ports of Dyea or Skagway (originally Skaguay). They then had to take the Chilkoot or White Pass trails to the Yukon River. At this point, they had to make themselves a boat and sail downriver to the Klondike. The Canadian government made the gold diggers bring a year's supply of food with them. This meant they had a heavy load to carry, so it was very difficult and not everybody reached the mines.

Historic miner's cabin.

Miners outside a gold mine.

The Chilkoot Trail

This was the most direct overland route to get to the main area of the goldfields around Dawson City and the Yukon River. It was also one of the cheapest ways to get there, so it became very popular. Those who chose the Chilkoot Trail started their journey from Dyea. This route was shorter than the others, but it was also more difficult because it was very steep.

The White Pass

This other main route left from Skagway harbor. It was longer than the Chilkoot Trail, but it wasn't as hard. This mountain pass, which still exists today, goes through the mountains which border Alaska and Canada. It starts from Skagway, Alaska, and leads to the lakes at the headwaters of the Yukon River.

Task

Internet research.

In 1848 another Gold Rush started in California. Find out:

- how long it lasted
- how many gold-seekers were involved
- what its long-term effects were

Test Yourself

Choose A, B or C to complete the sentences.

1 At the start of the story, Buck lived in an area good for
A ☑ agriculture **B** ☐ industry **C** ☐ oil

2 The gardener's helper who sold Buck was called
A ☐ Matthew **B** ☐ Martin **C** ☐ Manuel

3 Perrault and François worked for the ______ government.
A ☐ French **B** ☐ Canadian **C** ☐ United States

4 Which dog had only one eye?
A ☐ Dave **B** ☐ Sol-leks **C** ☐ Billee

5 What did Buck steal from Perrault and François one night when he was very hungry?
A ☐ fish **B** ☐ chicken **C** ☐ bacon

6 Spitz killed a _______ that Buck and the other dogs had wanted to catch.
A ☐ rabbit **B** ☐ wolf **C** ☐ moose

7 François and Perrault sold Buck and their dog-team to a man from
A ☐ England **B** ☐ America **C** ☐ Scotland

8 What did Hal carry with him?
A ☐ a hatchet **B** ☐ a knife **C** ☐ a book

9 Hal and Charles started their journey with
A ☐ ten dogs **B** ☐ twelve dogs **C** ☐ fourteen dogs

10 When did they first arrive at John Thornton's camp?
A ☐ spring **B** ☐ summer **C** ☐ autumn

11 At the end, Buck goes and lives with
A ☐ the Yeehats **B** ☐ the wolves **C** ☐ Judge Miller's family.

Syllabus

This reader contains the items listed below as well as those included in Levels A1 and A2.

Topics
Adventure
Betrayal
Courage
Respect
Love
The Wild

Connectives
so that, (in order) to
so, so...that, such...that
if
although, while,

Nouns
Countable and uncountable nouns with *some* and *any*
Abstract nouns
Compound nouns
Complex noun phrases

Verbs
Present Simple: including verbs not normally used in the continuous form; Present Continuous; Past Simple; Past Continuous; Past Perfect Simple: narrative, reported speech; Futures with Present Continuous, *going to* and *will*; modals: *could, must.*

Verb Forms and Patterns
Affirmative, interrogative, negative; Imperatives; Infinitives (with and without to) after verbs and adjectives; verb + *-ing* after verbs and prepositions; Gerunds as subjects and objects; Passive forms: Present Simple and Past simple

Functions
Discussing topics by asking and answering questions
Expressing personal opinion
Giving details of plans
Giving explanations

Stage 1

Charles Dickens, *Oliver Twist*
Maureen Simpson, *In Search of a Missing Friend*
Mark Twain, *A Connecticut Yankee in King Arthur's Court*
Lucy Maud Montgomery, *Anne of Green Gables*
E.A. Poe, *The Narrative of Arthur Gordon Pym of Nantucket*

Stage 2

Maria Luisa Banfi, *A Faraway World*
Frances Hodgson Burnett, *The Secret Garden*
Mary Flagan, *The Egyptian Souvenir*
Robert Louis Stevenson, *Treasure Island*
Mark Twain, *The Avventures of Tom Sawyer*

Stage 3

Charles Dickens, *David Copperfield*
Anonimous, *Robin Hood*
Mary Flagan, *Val's Diary*
Maureen Simpson, *Destination Karminia*
Jack London, *The Call of the Wild*